The Story
of the
Boston
Tea Party

The Story
of the
Boston
Tea Party

Mary Kay Phelan
drawings by Frank Aloise

Thomas Y. Crowell Company New York

Library of Congress Cataloging in Publication Data
Phelan, Mary Kay.
    The story of the Boston Tea Party.
    SUMMARY: Traces the causes and events of the
deliberately planned and carefully executed Boston Tea
Party.
    Bibliography: p.
    1. Boston Tea Party, 1773—Juv. lit.
[1. Boston Tea Party, 1773]   I. Aloise, Frank E.,
illus.   II.   Title.
E215.7.P45   973.3'115   72–7554
ISBN 0–690–77653–5

Especially
for
Richard Scott Phelan

By the Author:

Acknowledgment

Most historians agree that the Boston Tea Party was the decisive act which led to an open break with England. Eighteen months later the American Revolution began. What happened on the night of December 16, 1773, was not a sudden and irresponsible raid executed by fanatics. The patriot leaders had shown great patience in trying to find a peaceful way to resolve the tea crisis. Logic and reason prevailed throughout the many meetings. Only as a last resort did they turn to the tea party tactics.

Boston newspapers of 1773, diaries, journals, private correspondence, contemporary accounts by participants in the tea party, and minutes of the tea meeting as recorded in Proceedings of the Massachusetts Historical Society have been invaluable in writing this story. All quotations are taken from original sources. No conversation has been fictionalized.

Contents

The Story
of the
Boston
Tea Party

1
Secret
Session

Whisperings of unrest have been filling the crooked cobblestoned streets of Boston these past few weeks. Something is brewing. The town buzzes with rumors and suspicions. Around the tables in the Bunch of Grapes Tavern and the Crown Coffee House men are speculating about what will happen next. Everyone knows it all hinges on the Tea Act which the British Parliament passed last May.

Over at the office of the *Boston Gazette* on this night of October 16, 1773, the tiny paned windows have been tightly shuttered. Situated just behind the Town House, the building at the corner of Queen Street and Dassett Alley is occupied by the town's most powerful newspaper. There are others, of course—the *Massachusetts Spy*, the *Evening Post*, *Weekly Post-Boy*, and the Boston *News-Letter*. But none has the wide readership that the *Gazette* can claim. Opposing factions have nicknamed it "The Weekly Dung Barge"; Governor Hutchinson calls it "that infamous paper." Nevertheless, the publication has many loyal subscribers.

Ever since Benjamin Edes and John Gill ferried across the river from nearby Charlestown and set up their little print shop in 1755, the editors of the *Gazette* have been fearless in their writings. Criticism of royal officials and their policies has filled its pages; news has become secondary. Advertisements announcing the sale of goods newly arrived from foreign ports usually take up the greater part of the front page. But most readers turn to the second page first to read the political articles.

During the past few years, as quarrels with Great Britain have become more intense, the colonists divided into two groups. Those who are loyal to the King are known as Tories, while those who want to protect their rights and freedoms as individuals are called Whigs or patriots.

Benjamin Edes, an ardent patriot, has offered Whig leaders the second floor of his print shop as a meeting place for secret sessions. Here, uninterrupted and without fear of being overheard, they express their opinions, voice their hopes, and make plans for the future. Occasionally they contribute articles for the newspaper, signed with such names as "X," "Candidus," "Populus," and "Determinatus"—names which conceal the identity of the writer.

Anger toward Great Britain has been building up over the last ten years. It began soon after the French and Indian War ended. The victorious British had ousted the French from Canada. However, after the jubilation quieted down, Parliament was faced with the fact that war was an expensive business. To help meet the many debts, King George III decided the American colonists must be taxed.

The colonists hated the idea of taxes levied by a Parliament three thousand miles away. It was unfair. It was "taxation without representation," they argued, "and taxation without representation is tyranny."

Message after message was dispatched to King George. Could the colonies send representatives to Parliament? They, too, were Englishmen. They, too, had rights. But their pleas were ignored.

The first tax, the Stamp Act, took effect during November 1765. All newspapers were required to have a royal stamp. The press reacted violently, calling it a direct assault on their freedom. Benjamin Edes replaced the King's insignia on the front page of the *Gazette* with the drawing of a skull and crossbones. Furthermore, it was decreed that all business papers—notes and bonds, ships' clearance papers, property deeds, bills of lading, and wills—must have a stamp. Otherwise, no business transaction was legal.

The furious protests sent across the Atlantic brought

results. The hated Stamp Act was repealed less than five months later. But it was replaced by the Townshend Revenue Act, which levied a tax on paint and paper as well as on glass and tea. Resentment mounted. Mass meetings were held and the people were urged not to buy anything imported from England that was taxed.

As the months passed, English merchants found they were losing money. Trade between England and the colonies was practically at a standstill. They began pressuring King George III and Parliament to lift the taxes. Long and heated discussions followed. Finally, in December 1770, a bill was passed to eliminate all taxes, except a very small tax on tea.

Again the colonists were not to be fooled. If the king thought he could make them forget they were being taxed without representation, he was mistaken. Many people stubbornly refused to buy any tea imported from England. The *Gazette* called it "a nauseous draught," "vile growth," "the detestable weed."

Groups of Boston women organized non-tea parties and many of them signed an agreement to "deny ourselves the drinking of foreign tea, in hopes to frustrate a plan that tends to deprive a whole community of all that is valuable in life."

The pleasures of tea drinking, however, were well established. Some of the colonists continued to buy English tea and pay the duty. Then enterprising colonial merchants saw an opportunity to supply the beverage without paying a tax. They simply smuggled in tea from Holland. Those who used it said it was not only less expensive, it was better.

4

So, for the past three years, things have been relatively calm. Calm, that is, until news reached Boston in late August that Parliament had passed another Tea Act in May. Now there's a new controversy.

Tonight the first floor of the *Gazette* building is dark, the little handpress silent, the few fonts of type untouched. But on the second floor the flicker of candles is noted by those walking along the footways, although only shadowy outlines of men seated around a table can be detected. Yes, definitely, something is up!

The men meeting here call themselves The Long Room Club. No minutes are kept; everything that is said is considered strictly confidential. The acknowledged leader of the group is Sam Adams. His worn brown suit, spotted and stained, and his unkempt wig set askew on his head are mute testimony to Adams' indifference to appearances. His one purpose in life is to work for the individual rights and freedoms of the colonists; to him, nothing else matters.

Seated next to Adams is the merchant John Hancock. Wealthy and respected, he has only recently allied himself with the patriots' cause. Here, too, are Dr. Joseph Warren, who has managed to combine a successful medical practice with an enthusiasm for politics. William Cooper, a dedicated Whig and for many years Boston's efficient town clerk; the Reverend Samuel Cooper, his brother, who is minister of the Brattle Street Church; Paul Revere, a silversmith; and William Molineux, the hot-tempered Irish hardware merchant, who has vowed revenge on Parliament for his recent business failure.

Tonight's meeting has been called to discuss this

latest crisis—the insidious Tea Act. The group must decide what steps to take and how the *Gazette* can best further their purpose. Monday's paper will be printed tomorrow. The editorial should certainly voice their concern.

It was last January when the British East India Company found itself in trouble, grave trouble. In its London warehouses were seven years' accumulation of tea leaves. The colonists had refused to buy it. Instead, they were drinking tea smuggled into American ports on colonial merchant ships. If the tea were not purchased soon, it

would rot. And that would mean bankruptcy for one of England's most powerful companies. How could the American colonists be forced to buy the East India Company's product?

An appeal was made to Parliament and Crown officials devised a clever scheme. Heretofore, the East India Company had been required to pay export duty to English authorities before shipping tea to the American colonies. By eliminating this export duty, the price of tea could be cut in half. With the beverage now cheaper than that smuggled in from Holland, certainly the colonists would overlook the small three-pence-a-pound tax which Parliament insisted upon.

Also included in the plan was the stipulation that only certain agents, specifically chosen by the company, would be allowed to sell the tea in America. Thus the colonial merchants would be cut out of any trade. Everyone knows that the Boston agents selected by the company are notorious Tories. Once Parliament passed the Tea Act, hundreds of chests were loaded into ships bound for the ports of Philadelphia, New York, Charleston, and Boston.

During these past three years, Sam Adams had continued to protest the tax on tea. True, it was small. But to pay it, he argued, was an admission that Parliament had the right to tax the colonists. However, with everyone drinking the smuggled tea, most people had tended to listen to Adams with tolerant amusement.

Now, almost overnight, the situation has changed. The patriot leaders see financial ruin ahead for many of Boston's merchants. If certain Tories can be given a monopoly on the sale of tea, why not on other imports from England? There are woolens, glass, linens—all manner of goods manufactured in the mother country that Boston needs. Is this the beginning of a trend? A tax on one item can lead to another. Where will it stop?

The members of The Long Room Club have already heard that New York and Philadelphia are alert to the impending crisis. Patriots in these two cities are holding mass meetings to demand that the tea agents resign, that the ships sailing into port be forced to return to England without unloading the hated tea. However, no news has trickled in from Charleston, South Carolina.

Now, Boston must be aroused. Landing the tea can *not* be permitted. Instead, it must be sent back in the same ships in which it has arrived. How can the local agents be forced to give up their commissions?

As debate continues around the table, Benjamin Edes retires to one corner of the room. He will try to incorporate the opinions expressed here tonight in his Monday editorial. Another hour passes before he presents what he has written to The Long Room Club. Members nod approval as the printer reads:

October 18th   TO THE PUBLIC
 . . . Nothing can be more evident than their aim
to get all the trade and property in the empire into
their own power—their strides are large, numerous
and hasty; and if they are not vigorously opposed,
a community of noble, generous, and magnanimous
freemen will soon be reduced to a herd of miserable,
indigent, and spiritless slaves! Our expectations
of relief have been too long misplaced.

2
Old
Boston
Town

As the proud provincial capital of the Massachusetts Bay Colony, Boston is already an old community by New World standards. Governor John Winthrop and his hardy band of followers settled here in 1630. Now, as the principal port of New England, there are evidences on every side of prosperity. Most of the seventeen thousand people who live here are involved, one way or another, with its seagoing trade.

Because the town is almost entirely surrounded by water, it is termed geographically, a peninsula, the only connecting link to the mainland being a mile-long causeway called Boston Neck. When tides run high or rains are heavy, the causeway is sometimes covered with water, turning Boston into a true island.

Three sharp rises dominate the landscape—Trimontaine in the northwest, Copps Hill in the northeast, and Fort Hill near the eastern shore. Trimontaine is actually divided into three smaller hills—Beacon, Pemberton, and Mount Vernon. It is on Beacon Hill where the more prosperous residents have built their three-story mansions.

Just below Beacon Hill is the Common, some forty-eight acres purchased by the town more than one hundred years ago. The colonial militia trains here. People bring their cows to graze here. It's a favorite place for youngsters' sleds in the winter, games of tag in the summer.

Viewed from any one of the three hilltops, the valleys below seem to be a forest of chimneys. Every house, no matter what size, is heated by one or more fireplaces. Most homes are built of wood and jammed close together, fronting directly on the street. Windows are few because glass is imported from England, and the tax makes it an expensive luxury.

All traffic approaches from the south, coming in across Boston Neck and through the double-arched Town Gate. Pedestrians enter on one side; wagons, carts, and horseback riders pass through the other. Guards are on duty day and night, ready to stop anyone who acts in a suspicious manner.

Orange Street, leading in from the Town Gate, is

rough and unpaved. As the land broadens east and west, Orange Street becomes Newbury and then Marlborough. Since there are few house numbers, renaming a street every short distance is a common practice.

At the corner of Milk Street and Marlborough stands the Old South Meeting House, a sturdy brick structure, severely plain in design. The building's most prominent feature is the tall wooden steeple rising high above the street. Although primarily a church, Old South is sometimes used for political meetings because it can accommodate several thousand people, more than any other place in Boston.

At Old South the street name Marlborough becomes Cornhill, and terminates at the head of the broad thoroughfare known as King Street. This is probably the busiest street in town, always clogged with wagons, carts, and drays rumbling down and back from Long Wharf. The wharf itself is simply an extension of King Street, jutting half a mile into the water.

On the north side of Long Wharf are warehouses, shops, sail lofts, and the countinghouses of prosperous merchants. A roadway runs down the center, while on the open south side the world's largest ships can dock at low tide. The wharf is indeed an amazing engineering feat. Built some sixty years ago, it is still the pride of all Boston.

At the head of King Street stands the handsome two-story brick Town House. The lower floor forms the Royal Exchange, where colonial merchants meet every weekday at one o'clock to do their trading, in imitation of the London Exchange. The upper floor has been designated as "the seat of government" for the colony. The

Royal Governor has an office here. Crown officials trans-
act business in the Council Chamber and elected representatives for the province meet in the Assembly Hall.

Soaring high above the second floor is the clock
tower, flanked on either side by statues of the lion and
unicorn. On "rejoicing days," when a particular act of
tyranny has been repealed by Parliament, the tower is
illuminated with hundreds of candles.

Nearby is noisy Dock Square, shadowed by the imposing Faneuil Hall, two-and-a-half stories high and built
of brick. It was presented to Boston thirty years ago by a
wealthy merchant, Peter Faneuil. The open-arched lower
floor is designed as a marketplace. Here Boston house-
wives flock to buy their fresh foods, choosing from the
piles of cabbages, corn, pumpkins; the rows and rows of
plucked turkeys and hens; the wooden casks of butter
and cheeses. Farmers who own slaves often send them
in to haggle prices with the buyers. Dock Square echoes
with shouts and laughter.

On the second floor of Faneuil Hall is a spacious
room, large enough to seat a thousand people. Town meetings are held here. In addition, there are various other
rooms where civic groups gather. Above the cupola is a
grasshopper weathervane, the work of Shem Drowne,
well-known coppersmith. Rumor has it that Drowne chose
this particular insect because, while chasing one as a
small boy, he met the man who started him on the road
to success.

The details of the copper grasshopper are remark-
ably intricate; the glass eyes sparkle and glint in bright
sunlight. When a seaman comes into Boston and tries to

claim residence here, the authorities often ask, "What's on top of Faneuil Hall?" Unless he can answer "A grasshopper," the questioners know the seaman is not a resident.

Skirting the eastern shoreline of the town is a mass of piers, shipyards, warehouses, and wharves, for Boston is a community almost entirely dependent upon the sea. The harbor swarms with tall-masted merchant vessels, whalers, sloops and schooners, ferries, and fishing ketches. More than anything else, these ships symbolize the town's prosperity.

During the daylight hours there are a thousand discordant sounds along the waterfront. Some five hundred vessels clear the port of Boston each year. The screech of winches, the thud of barrels, the shouts of dock workers loading and unloading cargo—this noisy pandemonium fascinates newcomers.

There is little by way of formal entertainment in the town. Theaters are forbidden and visiting groups of players discouraged. The men find their relaxation in the taverns and coffeehouses where, night after night, they gather around the long tables to discuss politics while smoking their pipes, drinking their rum punch. From the wealthiest merchant to the poorest dock worker, each has one or two favorite meeting places where he can usually be found between supper and bedtime.

For the women there are few diversions, other than reading or writing letters. A proper lady even hesitates to go to the meetinghouse without an escort. In recent years, however, a new entertainment has been introduced. It's become "a polite custom" to ask Mrs. John Wheatley to bring her Phillis for a poetry session.

Eleven years ago Mrs. Wheatley bought the little black slave girl at a market auction. She was a wisp of a child, probably five or six years old. The Wheatleys soon found that Phillis was unusually gifted. Under their gentle training she has become a soft-voiced, modest young woman. Though Phillis was given her freedom in 1771, she has remained with the family and they have continued to encourage her talent for writing. Boston matrons these days enjoy hearing Phillis read the beautiful poems she has composed. They often request the eloquent and moving one she wrote about her own heritage:

Should you, my lords while you peruse my song,
Wonder from whence my love of Freedom sprung,
Whence flow these wishes for the common good,
By feeling hearts alone best understood,
I, young in life, by seeming cruel fate
Was snatched from Afric's distant happy seat;
Steeled was that soul and by no misery moved
That from a mother seized her babe beloved:
Such was my case. And can I then but pray
Others may never feel tyrannic sway?

Many people say that Boston's most familiar sound is one of bells. Tower bells from the town's sixteen churches ring out furiously for fires, toll solemnly for funerals. Everyone recognizes the "royal peal" of the eight bells of Christ's Church, the off-key sounds of New North, the deep slow tones of King's Chapel.

Markets are opened and closed by the bells. On Sundays they ring twice, once in the morning and again in the afternoon, calling everyone to church. During the week, town meetings are announced by the bells. Then there are the noisy little hand bells that street peddlers ring to advertise their wares. Tavern owners proclaim that meals are served by clanging their bells. Schoolmasters ring sharply to call their charges into the classrooms. And everywhere there's the musical tinkle of door bells in hundreds of shops and homes.

After the curfew is rung at nine o'clock each night, householders lock their doors and shutter their windows. While all Boston sleeps, the town crier paces through the crooked streets, calling out the time and the weather.

3
The
Tories'
Dilemma

Set back from the commotion of Marlborough Street is the massive three-story Province House, residence of the Royal Governor. The spacious grounds are filled with towering elms and surrounded by an ornamental iron fence. A cobblestone driveway leads up to the portico of the square brick house. Visitors are impressed with the British coat of arms mounted over the palatial doorway—a lion and unicorn elaborately carved and gilded. The casual passerby usually glances up to the lofty cupola to find out which way the wind blows. A hammered copper figure with drawn bow and arrow serves as a weathervane.

For the past three years Thomas Hutchinson has occupied the official residence, ever since he replaced Francis Bernard as Royal Governor of the Massachusetts Bay Colony. Hutchinson, a native-born American, proudly traces his ancestry back through several generations to one of Boston's oldest and wealthiest families. After graduating from Harvard, he turned to politics, becoming as active as had been his father and grandfather before him.

The offices which Thomas Hutchinson has held have all been "by royal appointment." His sympathies have always been allied with Great Britain. Yet as an official of the King he likes to think he is friendly with those he calls "the commonality"—but only so long as that commonality keeps its place. And that place is far beneath the colonial aristocrat.

Hutchinson's high-handed attitude toward the Whigs has long been a source of irritation to Sam Adams. In fact, he dislikes the man intensely, seeing him as a grasping, avaricious Tory whose only ambition is pleasing King George III. For this reason Adams has used every tactic he can devise to discredit the governor in the eyes of the local citizenry.

On this Monday afternoon, October 18, Governor Hutchinson is in his study at Province House chatting with John Singleton Copley, Boston's most famous portrait artist. Copley has just finished a portrait of the governor and Hutchinson is obviously pleased with the result.

A tall handsome figure looks out from the canvas. The eyes are hazel, the complexion fair, the features delicate. Copley seems to have caught both grace and pride in the erect stature of his subject; yet overall there are those qualities of self-confidence and aloofness, so well known to the governor's contemporaries.

The men's conversation is interrupted by a knock on the study door. The governor strides across the room to open it. His secretary stands there with a copy of today's *Boston Gazette* in hand. Here's an editorial, he says, which he thinks his employer should see.

Glancing down the column, Thomas Hutchinson frowns. ". . . Nothing can be more evident than their aim to get all the trade and property in the empire into their own power. . . ." So, the radical press is trying to blow up the simple Tea Act into a controversy! He decides that he should consult with the tea agents immediately and directs that a messenger be sent to the homes of these men, asking them to come to Province House this evening.

Turning back to his guest, the governor explains what has happened. Although Copley was reared in a Whig atmosphere, he is the son-in-law of one of the tea agents. He has friends among both Whigs and Tories. As an artist he has no interest in politics and has remained nonpartisan these past few years. Now he suggests he should be leaving. The governor shows him to the door and thanks him for the excellent job he has done on the portrait.

By seven o'clock the candles in every room on the first floor of the mansion are lighted. Governor Hutchinson awaits the arrival of the agents with some impatience.

A clatter of carriage wheels on the private driveway hurries him to the front door. Warmly he greets his sons, Thomas and Elisha. The press sometimes makes disparaging remarks about "the Children," because Hutchinson has used his influence in London to have them appointed by the East India Company. There are rumors that the governor himself has a financial interest in their tea business, though no one has ever been able to prove it.

Within minutes a second carriage draws up, bringing Richard Clarke and his son, Isaac. These two, together with a second son, Jonathan, compose the firm of Richard Clarke & Sons. For the past ten years they have been Boston's major importers of tea, which they sell in their store at the foot of King Street. The Clarkes and the Hutchinsons are old friends. The families have been even closer since young Thomas married Mr. Clarke's daughter.

When the governor asks about Jonathan, he is told that the young man is still in London. There were verbal orders, of course, appointing the agents, but no formal papers have yet been drawn up. Jonathan's mission is to secure those papers. He should be back by mid-November, Mr. Clarke adds.

It is not long before the other two agents, Edward Winslow and Benjamin Faneuil, join the group. The governor suggests they follow him into the study where they can discuss the situation which confronts them.

Once the men are comfortably seated, Thomas Hutchinson admits he is disturbed by today's editorial in the *Gazette*. How do the others feel?

Richard Clarke takes out a letter he has just written to a friend in London. Adjusting his glasses, he explains that this communication best expresses his sentiments. He reads:

> What difficulties may arise from the disaffection of the merchants and importers of tea to this measure of the East India Company, I am not yet able to say. It seems at present to be a matter of much speculation, and if one is to credit the prints, no small opposition will be made thereto . . . . My friends seem to think it will subside; others are of a contrary opinion.

The agents nod in agreement. No one has really been concerned until recently. Now they wonder if a crisis can be brewing.

Hutchinson warns of the growing power of what he calls the "extra-legal groups" in town. Especially distasteful to him are the Sons of Liberty, a semi-secret organization that Sam Adams started five years ago. When gangs of high-spirited young men from the North End began fighting with other gangs from the South End, Adams saw a great opportunity. Quietly he welded the two groups together. Now these Sons of Liberty are ready to harass the Tories in any way their leader suggests.

In addition, there are the caucuses—political clubs sponsored by the patriots. They seem to take matters into their own hands and ignore all directives from the governor. Although membership in these caucuses includes citizens from all parts of Boston, certain Whig leaders show up at every meeting. Hutchinson admits that his Tory friends tell him the influence of these groups is strong. They may even attempt to challenge the power of the Royal government. And that, says the governor doubling his fist for emphasis, must never be allowed to happen. Never!

Richard Clarke asks about the men appointed as the East India Company agents in New York and Philadelphia. He's heard there is a movement afoot to force their resignations. And what about the tea that is supposed to land in Charleston, South Carolina? Is anything being done there?

Hutchinson shrugs off the question. Let those three port cities handle their own problems. Here in Boston he will give his full support to the tea agents, he promises, in their efforts to carry out the plans of the London company. There's Castle William, of course—the fortress island three miles below Boston—where a regiment of British soldiers is stationed.

The *Active* and the *Kingfisher*, His Majesty's men-of-war, ride at anchor nearby. Certainly the soldiers and the ships should be sufficient to suppress any uprising or mob violence.

The governor's confidence is reassuring. The agents promise they will do nothing further until their written orders from London arrive.

Thomas Hutchinson accompanies his guests to the door and shakes hands cordially with the men as they file out to the waiting carriages. Returning to his study, he pulls out a folder from his desk drawer, rereading the letter on top.

Here it is: the permission he has sought from Crown officials in London. Several months ago the governor decided to ask for a leave of absence. He was weary of all the harassment by local Whig leaders. The publication of some private correspondence was the final insult—a deliberate intent to smear his character. But that was before the controversy over the tea tax had arisen.

Thomas Hutchinson, despite his many failings, is a proud and conscientious man. Perhaps even stubborn. He has no intention of quitting under fire. Too many of his Tory friends and their fortunes are involved. Meticulously, he replaces the letter of permission in its folder.

The leave of absence can wait. He intends to win this showdown with the patriots before temporarily retiring from his duties as governor.

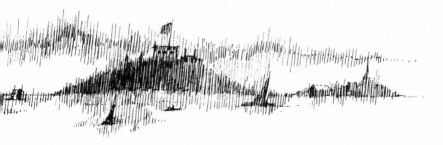

4
Patriot
Leader

It is now three days since
Benjamin Edes' editorial appeared. As Sam Adams snuffs
out the last candle in the second floor room of Faneuil
Hall, a broad smile spreads across his face. It's a strong
face. The eyes are steel gray, the nose is long and rather
full, the lips thin but the expression kindly. Though usually soft-spoken, the patriot is not a gentle person when
action is needed. Tonight was just such a time; the meet-

ing with the Committee of Correspondence has been a success. He is particularly grateful for the active support and assistance of a native New Yorker, Dr. Thomas Young, a physician who moved to Boston only seven years ago. Now Adams has been asked to write to the outlying towns, telling them of the current tea controversy.

People in Boston often wonder about Sam Adams. How his wife, Betsy, manages to feed and clothe her family is something of a mystery. Ever since graduation from Harvard, Adams has tried one job after another—and failed. His small inheritance from his father's estate has dwindled to almost nothing.

Though he has never been successful in business ventures—and cares less—he is a master of political maneuver. Adams knows the citizens of Boston as no other man does—their politics, their reliability as Whigs or Tories. For the past ten years he's been frequenting the taverns, joining at least a dozen different groups every day to talk politics. He's skillful in influencing their thinking, never pushing an argument too far, but quietly encouraging opposition to Parliament's assaults on the colonists' freedoms. Slowly, carefully Sam Adams has been building the patriot cause, drawing into it whomever he can persuade.

One of the converts is his second cousin, John Adams, thirteen years younger than Sam. John has recently moved to Boston from his small farm in neighboring Braintree. He finds it more convenient to carry on his law practice here.

John and his wife, Abigail, are living in a little house

over on Queen Street. Sam has made it a habit to drop in
on them often to talk politics. John's logical mind and his
blunt honesty make these discussions a pleasure, though
the lawyer favors gradual change rather than any sudden
upheaval. At times he seems too cautious to satisfy his
more radical cousin. Nevertheless, Sam is convinced that
John will support the patriots' cause when the time comes
for action.

Tonight, groping his way down the darkened stair-
case, the patriot leader steps out into the narrow street. He
pauses to glance back at ornate Faneuil Hall. Here are
conducted all town meetings—the democratic institutions
so peculiar to the New England colonies. Here is the very
essence of liberty, where each man can speak out without
fear of reprisal. It's in town meetings, too, that the Board
of Selectmen are chosen, the officials who manage Boston's
affairs.

Admittedly, King George III still maintains a certain
control over the Massachusetts Bay Colony. He appoints
the governor, the lieutenant-governor, and the secretary
of the province. But members of the legislature are
elected by the people in a town meeting. The upper house
is known as the Council; the lower house, the Assembly.
Members of the Council are selected by the Assembly,
though the governor is privileged to veto any choice, and
often does.

Each town in the colony sends at least one representative to the Assembly. Boston has four, and Sam Adams
is proud that he is now one of these lawmakers. Before
reporting to the annual assembly, every representative is
instructed in the issues his community wishes him to

support. If something unexpected arises, bells are rung for another town meeting and new instructions are given. Thus, each town keeps a tight rein on its legislators.

At this moment Sam Adams is wondering which way to walk home. Along the waterfront, he decides. It's his favorite route. As a boy he had scampered up and down these piers, watching workmen unload cargo from ships sailing in from faraway lands. During the last few years he's made many friends here, too—dock workers, shipwrights, carpenters, sparmakers, caulkers. Often during the noon hour Adams wanders along the wharves, talking to anyone who will listen. His one theme is always how precious freedom is, how the British government must not infringe on the colonists' rights. And among these workingmen, he has found many recruits for the Sons of Liberty.

Striding on past Rowe's Wharf, Adams pulls the collar of his old red cloak tighter around his neck. There is a chill wind blowing in from the ocean, breaking huge waves against the shore line. Even the wind, however, does not dispel the pungent smells of a thriving port—the odor of tar and spices mingled with the tang of fresh fish and salt water.

After passing Griffin's Wharf, Sam Adams turns into Purchase Street. It is only a few steps to the old wooden house where he has lived all his fifty-one years. Rundown though it is, the patriot leader has neither the time nor money to make needed repairs. Anyway, he has never noticed.

When he opens the front door, the huge Newfoundland dog, Queue, bounds up to greet his master. The fire

on the hearth is almost out; it is evident that the family has already gone to bed. Tossing off the red cloak, Adams hurries over to the dilapidated desk in the corner. There is work to be done tonight. Letters must go out to the Committees of Correspondence in neighboring towns informing them of the tense situation now coming to a head.

How well he remembers that night in October last year when the idea of the Committees was born. He had gone down to Plymouth to visit James and Mercy Warren. In their comfortable two-story house, Sam Adams could relax. He was with friends. And he liked to gaze at the sturdy Pilgrim Rock, visible from the Warrens' garden. It gave him renewed vigor to see where the first Englishmen landed in Massachusetts Bay—those brave people who prized freedom above everything else.

Although a gentleman farmer by profession, James Warren was deeply interested in politics. His wife, Mercy Otis, had grown up in a household where ideas of liberty and independence predominated. Now a writer of brilliant satires, she had found great stimulation in conversations with Sam Adams.

Leading the fireside conclave, Mercy had suggested letter writing as a possible way to bring the people in surrounding towns closer together. During that evening the scheme of Committees of Correspondence was hatched. Committees would be appointed throughout the province to correspond with each other regarding grievances and future plans. Yes, Adams believed it would work.

He had returned to Boston, and on November 2,

1772, had succeeded in calling a special town meeting. Facing the crowd in Faneuil Hall, he had explained his idea. Boston citizens, he said, knew what was going on, what was being done to preserve their liberties. But in the smaller outlying communities, the villagers heard little. Why not keep them better informed?

"I move," said Adams, "that a Committee of Correspondence be appointed, to consist of twenty-one persons, to state the rights of the colonists and of this province in particular, and to communicate and publish the same to the several towns, with the infringements and violations thereof that have been, or from time to time may be, made."

The motion had been unanimously adopted and the following night members of the committee began drafting letters. Before long, replies came back from the various towns. They liked the idea. They were forming committees of their own. This method of transmitting views was proving most effective. At first the documents had been circulated only in Massachusetts Bay, but it was not long before committees were spreading to other colonies.

Writing letters is not easy for Sam Adams. Now that he is getting older, his hand shakes even more with the palsy that plagues him. No matter. Tonight he grasps the quill pen with trembling fingers and begins a letter to the committee in Roxbury; then to Dorchester, Brookline, and Cambridge.

After summarizing the current situation, he adds: "It is easy to see how aptly this scheme will serve both to destroy the trade of the colonies and increase the revenue. How necessary then it is that each colony should take effectual methods to prevent this measure from having its designed effects."

There, the last letter is finished. As Sam Adams begins sealing the documents with his wax stamp, he hears a voice outside. It's the town crier, shuffling along the brick footway.

"Half after eleven o'clock," he calls, "and a fine clear night. All is well."

All is well? The patriot shakes his head.

5
Liberty
Tree
Ultimatum

I t is very apparent that the Whig leaders are using every means possible to arouse the citizenry. In the October 25 issue of the *Gazette,* Benjamin Edes and John Gill publish a scorching editorial addressed:

TO THE COMMISSIONERS
APPOINTED BY THE EAST INDIA COMPANY
FOR THE SALE OF TEA IN AMERICA

. . . The claim of Parliament to tax America, has been too well examined for *you* to doubt, at this time, to which side right and justice have given the palm. Do not, therefore, hesitate at the course you ought to pursue. If you deliberate, you are lost—lost to virtue, lost to your country.

It is in vain to expect that Americans can give sanction to your office—FREEMEN—AMERICAN FREEMEN can never approve it. You are abundantly capable to judge for yourselves. And I sincerely wish that your conduct in the present alarming occasion, may be such as will promote your future peace and welfare. It is in your power and *you are now warned of it,* to save yourselves much Trouble, and secure your native country from the deadly Stroke now aimed in your persons against her.

Again on November 1, the *Gazette* comes out with a blistering attack on the governor. Though it is written under the pen name of "Praedicus," most people guess that it is Sam Adams who has composed the article. In part it reads:

TO MR. HUTCHINSON

. . . Sir, of this you may rest assured, that the opposition will hardly subside while a single farthing is by any means extorted from us without our consent . . . The clamor against the tea is not as an article of trade but as a commodity that British ministry have infected with the plague . . . don't you begin to tremble, Mr. Hutchinson?

Meanwhile, over at the Green Dragon Tavern on Union Street, the North End Caucus is holding meeting after meeting. "We were so careful," wrote Paul Revere, "that our meetings should be kept secret, that every time we met, every person swore upon the Bible not to discover any of our transactions." It was just five days ago that the membership voted "to oppose the vending of any Tea, sent by the East India Company to any part of the Continent, with our lives and fortunes."

Now, on this evening of November 2, Dr. Joseph Warren is chosen to preside at the caucus. Sam Adams is there, sitting quietly on the back row, but nodding vigorous assent as Dr. Warren announces that the time for direct action has come. Tirades in the newspapers seem to have had no effect. The tea agents must be made to resign their commissions—and in public.

It is decided to hold a mass meeting under the Liberty Tree at noon tomorrow. The towering elm in Hanover Square has been a gathering spot for patriot activities ever since the Stamp Act was defied. It seems an appropriate place to meet the agents. They will be directed to appear at twelve o'clock.

Benjamin Edes, who is also present tonight, volunteers to print handbills announcing the assembly, which can be posted throughout the town. Will the members of the caucus trust his judgment in composing the handbill? he asks.

Approval is given and the printer excuses himself from the group. He must start at once, he explains, if the posters are to be ready early tomorrow morning.

Before the meeting is formally adjourned, the resolutions summoning the tea agents are drafted by Dr. Joseph Warren and Dr. Thomas Young. Several members offer to deliver them to the tea agents before the night is over.

It is nearly one o'clock in the morning when Richard Clarke is aroused by violent knocking on the front door of his house in School Street. Looking out the bedroom window, he sees two men standing in the courtyard below. They shout that they have an important message. Sleepily, Mr. Clarke gropes his way down the stairs and takes the paper handed to him. With astonishment he reads that he is commanded "to make a public resignation of your commission" at noon under the Liberty Tree. "Fail not upon your peril," the writer warns. Identical notifications are delivered in the early morning hours to the other agents.

November 3 dawns clear, although there is a sharp wind blowing in across the bay. The handbills printed in the *Gazette* shop are already posted all over town. Citizens scurrying through the streets on their way to work read this surprising message:

TO THE FREEMEN OF THIS AND NEIGHBORING TOWNS:
Gentlemen:
You are desired to meet at Liberty Tree this day at 12 o'clock noon; then and there to hear the persons, to whom the tea shipped by the East India Company is consigned, make a public resignation of their office as Consignees, upon oath; and also swear that they will reship any teas that may be consigned to them by said Company, by the first vessel sailing for London.
Boston, Nov. 3, 1773

O.C.
Secretary
Show us the man that dare take this down.

Soon after eleven o'clock, bells in the church steeples all over town begin ringing wildly, persistently. Criers roam through the streets summoning everyone to come to the Liberty Tree. Carpenters drop their tools, blacksmiths leave their forges, countinghouse clerks put down their quill pens and run out to join the crowds hurrying along the footways leading to the Liberty Tree. Merchants, who fear there may be disturbances, shutter their shop windows and lock the doors.

Meanwhile, the tea agents are gathering at the warehouse of Richard Clarke & Sons on Long Wharf. The men appear shaken by the peremptory summons, but none is ready to give in to the patriots' demands. They are apprehensive that something unpleasant is about to happen; together they can give each other support.

Out in the harbor the King's men-of-war are riding at anchor, their great black hulls encircled by broad yellow bands. Young Thomas Hutchinson reminds the men that the ships' guns are pointed toward the shore line, that his father has assured them this is protection enough.

By noon there are some five hundred people assembled under the great elm in Hanover Square. More and more keep coming. The patriot leaders make speeches while they wait for the tea agents to appear; by twelve-thirty not one has shown up. Sam Adams asks John Hancock and Dr. Warren to step aside for a moment. Should they put a resolution before this crowd? he asks. The other two agree.

Adams holds up his hand for silence. Is it the wish of those assembled here to send a committee to the agents and demand their resignations? There is a roar of approval. If they refuse, continues Adams, should they be declared enemies of their country?

"Yes! Yes! Yes!"

William Molineux is appointed to lead a delegation of nine men down King Street to Clarke's warehouse where it's rumored the agents are secluded. Most of the crowd follows along behind. As they pass the Town House, Governor Hutchinson is standing beside an upstairs window. Earlier in the day he had called a special session of the Council "to help preserve peace," but no one had appeared. Now, watching the procession, the governor admits to his secretary that there are many "better-class citizens" in the company.

When they reach Long Wharf, the spectators stop at the edge and watch while the nine men approach the warehouse. Molineux bangs on the door. Several minutes pass before Richard Clarke opens it.

"From whom are you a committee?" inquires Mr. Clarke.

"From the whole people," Molineux replies.

"Who are the committee?"

"I am one," says Molineux and names the others: William Dennie, Dr. Joseph Warren, Dr. Benjamin Church, Henderson Inches, Edward Proctor, Nathaniel Barber, Gabriel Johonnot, and Ezekiel Cheever.

"What is your request?" demands Clarke, his voice edged with irritation.

"That you give us your word to sell none of the teas in your charge, but to return them to London in the same bottoms in which they were shipped. Will you comply?"

"I shall have nothing to do with you," snaps Clarke.

Molineux then withdraws a sheet of paper from his pocket, explaining that certain resolutions have been passed at the Liberty Tree. If the agents refuse to comply, they are "enemies to their country and shall be dealt with accordingly."

A long silence follows. Mr. Clarke glares at the committee members. It is evident that the agents will not budge from their original position. The delegation stalks out of the warehouse.

When the waiting crowd learns the results of the encounter, there is a menacing roar. "Out with them, out with them!" many shout. Several high-spirited young men rush toward the building and begin wrenching the doors off their hinges.

The agents, now thoroughly frightened, flee to the second floor countingroom and bar the heavy door for protection. Molineux and his committee realize that mob action is not the answer . . . that violence will accomplish nothing. They step forward to block the way of the impetuous youths. Slowly the crowd begins to disperse.

It is several hours before the tea agents dare leave the warehouse. This has been their first experience with a mob of patriotic citizens. They are thoroughly shaken.

The next evening agent Benjamin Faneuil is startled by a harsh rap on the front door of his house on Tremont Street. Approaching cautiously, he discovers a letter has been slipped under the door. With trembling fingers he unfolds the paper. "Long has this people been irreconcilable to the idea of spilling human blood . . . ." he reads. "But," the writer goes on, "it was only recently that a common thief had been executed for his crime." Ominously the letter warns, "You boldly avow a resolution to bear a principal part in the robbery of every inhabitant of this country."

Is this a threat against his life? Faneuil pales at the thought. Are the patriots really so determined?

6
Tempest in Town Meeting

Sam Adams is proceeding with caution. Here, at last, is an issue that has the patriots thoroughly incensed. They are ready for action, but that action must be carefully planned. He wants no part of mob rule. The refusal of the tea agents to appear at the Liberty Tree was outright defiance, of course. But now a way must be found to force the agents to give up their commissions.

Together with other Whig leaders, Adams circulates a petition asking the Selectmen to call a town meeting. This is a legal procedure—all within the regulations of the local government.

On Friday morning, November 5, more than six hundred assemble in Faneuil Hall. They are the ministers of the meetinghouses, the doctors, lawyers, judges, town officials, and merchants, as well as sea captains, tavern keepers, and artisans. Now, gathered in a town meeting, these men are here to perform their civic duty.

John Hancock is chosen as moderator. From the rostrum he announces that the meeting has been called to decide what steps to take next in the tea controversy.

After an hour of deliberation it is again agreed that the sending of tea to America, subject to payment of duties on being landed in Boston, is "a violent attack upon the liberties of America" and it is "the duty of every American to oppose the attempt." A committee is appointed to make formal calls upon the tea agents, to ask once again for their resignations. The town meeting, says Mr. Hancock, will reconvene tomorrow morning to hear the replies.

As was to be expected, the tea agents continue to stall for time. All six refuse to comply with the town's request, saying they still do not know what terms have been made with the East India Company. They can do nothing until formal orders are received from London.

When these answers are reported to the group assembled in Faneuil Hall the next day, everyone is angered. Some speak of violence. Others suggest taking up arms, but the more level-headed leaders discourage such talk.

Instead, a resolution is passed to inform the agents that their answers are "daringly affrontive to the Town," and the meeting adjourns. Refusing to appear at the Liberty Tree last Wednesday was one thing, but now the agents have defied the request of a legal town meeting.

The next few days pass in deceptive quiet. The newspapers are filled with hostile articles; letters to the editors continue to berate the tea agents. Rumors circulate around town that the governor has ordered a company of soldiers to come in from Castle William but no one can prove anything. Someone starts the story that small groups have been assigned to kidnap the agents. Nothing happens.

On Wednesday, November 17, comes positive word that the tea ships are on their way. Captain James Scott is bringing his vessel into Boston harbor, laden with cargo from London. He has refused the East India Company's request to carry any of the tea himself, but reports that three ships filled with tea chests left the English port at the same time he did. They are all bound for Boston, he says. It's disquieting news, though not unexpected.

One of the arrivals on Captain Scott's ship is young Jonathan Clarke. Everyone surmises that he has probably brought formal papers from the East India Company, giving the tea agents their specific orders. Word spreads rapidly. The patriots, acting quickly, call a town meeting for nine o'clock tomorrow morning.

At the appointed hour hundreds converge on Faneuil Hall. Sam Adams wastes no time in pointing out the specific dangers. Under no circumstances, he says, must the cargo from the tea ships be allowed to land. Once it is ashore and the duties paid, the patriots' protest against

the tax on tea will be a lost cause. Further, Adams continues, there is a rumor that the agents may propose that when the ships arrive, the tea will be stored in a customs warehouse until further instructions can be received from the East India Company. Such an idea is preposterous. Who can trust Governor Hutchinson or the customs officers? They would undoubtedly turn the tea over to the agents immediately.

There is only one solution. The patriots must make certain that the tea is returned in the same ships in which it arrives. And that, asserts Adams, can only be done by forcing the Tory agents to resign their commissions and refuse to claim the tea.

Another committee is appointed to call on the agents and once more request their resignations. Before dissolving the town meeting, the chairman announces they will reconvene this afternoon.

The message which the committee brings back is not surprising. It reads:

Boston, November 18, 1773

Sir—In answer to the message we have this day received from the town, we beg leave to say that we have not yet received any order from the East India Company respecting the expected teas, but we are now further acquainted that our friends in England have entered into general engagements in our behalf, merely of a commercial nature, which puts it out of our power to comply with the request of the town.

We are, sir, your most humble servants,
Richard Clarke & Sons
Benj. Faneuil, Jr. for self and Joshua Winslow, Esq.
Elisha Hutchinson, for my Brother and self.

Instead of the usual catcalls and cries of indignation which might have been expected, the men assembled accept the letter in grim silence. There is no debate, no comment. They simply move to adjourn.

Later that day the tea agents meet with Governor Hutchinson. They are thoroughly alarmed by reports of what has happened at the town meeting. Votes of censure they could understand, even condemnation. But the abrupt silence is mysterious. What new danger is impending?

The agents plead with the governor to take over the tea when the ships sail into Boston harbor. Wouldn't he be willing to shoulder the responsibility for them?

Even though he would like to do so, Governor Hutchinson replies, he must refuse. A royal governor is not in any position to take possession of the shipments from a private company. Besides, he adds, he is certain the patriots are only bluffing. After the twenty-day period, the royal customs men will move in and confiscate the chests. Then it will all be sold at public auction and the agents will be back in business without any financial loss whatsoever. Perhaps there will even be a profit, he adds slyly.

Nevertheless the visitors admit they are alarmed. The violence at Clarke's warehouse, the veiled threats of assassination, the continued pressure from the Whig newspapers—it's all very disturbing.

The governor suggests that perhaps the agents would prefer to move out to Castle William where they can be protected by the royal troops stationed there. The men eagerly accept this invitation. It's a cold and lonely place, but at least they and their families will be out of personal danger in these quarters.

Meanwhile, the second refusal of the tea agents to resign is precisely what Sam Adams had hoped for. This will give him time to get the surrounding communities more involved. As chairman of Boston's Committee of Correspondence, he sends letters to committee members in Roxbury, Dorchester, Brookline, Cambridge, and Charlestown asking them to meet with the Boston group on Monday, November 22.

Not one refuses the invitation. The Selectmen's chambers in Faneuil Hall are filled at the specified time. Enthusiasm runs high. The men from the outlying communities pledge themselves to resist any landing or sale of the tea. Sam Adams has prepared a letter to be sent throughout the province and he reads it aloud for the joint committees' approval:

> We think, gentlemen, that we are in duty bound to use our most strenuous endeavors to ward off the impending evil, and we are sure that upon a fair and cool inquiry into the nature and tendency of the ministerial plan, you will think this tea now coming to us more to be dreaded than plague and pestilence.

When Adams finishes, there is prolonged applause. The committees give hearty endorsement to the bold language. Adams smiles. How different this occasion is from previous crises when each community had been more or less isolated. Now there is a bond between them. Now they are pulling together.

Newspapers, too, continue to arouse the citizens. In

today's issue of the *Gazette*, printer Benjamin Edes has written a stirring editorial encouraging new defiance among those concerned with their liberties. He closes the article with a challenge:

> Americans! defeat this last effort of a most pernicious, expiring faction, and you may sit under your own vines and fig trees, and none shall, hereafter, dare to make you afraid!

7
The
Dartmouth
Arrives

It is Sunday, November 28. And Sunday in Boston is unlike any other day in the week. Everyone goes to church. There are two long sessions, one in the morning and another in the afternoon with a short break for lunch at twelve o'clock. Those who fail to attend church are fined. Any travel or transaction of business is illegal. Strolling through the streets or playing games on the Common is absolutely forbidden.

Early this morning a large sailing ship was sighted, threading its way cautiously through the narrow channel, almost brushing against the brass cannon mounted on Castle Island. It is not long before the news spreads like brushfire through the town. Ministers announce it from their pulpits, uttering lengthy prayers for the strength to continue the fight against taxation. The first of the hated tea ships has arrived. Captain James Hall is bringing the *Dartmouth* into the harbor after an eight-week passage from London. There are one hundred and fourteen tea chests in the ship's hold.

Here is a situation that demands immediate action. Under no circumstance must the cargo be allowed to land. Sabbath or no Sabbath, the Board of Selectmen meet in extraordinary session at noon, hoping they will have some word from the tea agents. Unless the officials have some new proposals to present, they cannot call a legal town meeting. No word comes; the agents are all unavailable.

Meanwhile, Sam Adams and Dr. Joseph Warren decide to take matters into their own hands. They call the Committee of Correspondence together and make plans for a mass meeting at Faneuil Hall tomorrow morning. Such a gathering suits the purposes of the patriots better, anyway.

Actual participation in a town meeting is restricted to qualified voters—those people who own property. Such voters number about twenty-five hundred in the town's population of seventeen thousand.

The Committee of Correspondence wants to broaden its base of opposition to the tea tax. In calling this mass meeting, where all the men of the town are welcome, the protest will become more widespread. Messages must be sent out tonight, inviting all the people in the surrounding communities as well.

Boston citizens awake on Monday morning to find their town plastered with placards which read:

FRIENDS! BRETHREN! GENTLEMEN!

That worst of plagues, the detested TEA, shipped for this port by the East India Company has now arrived in this harbor. The hour of destruction, or manly opposition to the machinations of tyranny, stares you in the face. Every friend to his country, to his posterity, is now called upon to meet at Faneuil Hall at nine o'clock THIS DAY (at which time the bells will ring), to make a united and successful resistance to this last, worst and most destructive measure of the Administration.

Church bells begin pealing out precisely at nine. People can be seen streaming along the narrow streets from every direction, all converging on Faneuil Hall. Jonathan Williams is elected moderator and William Cooper, the town clerk, is asked to keep the minutes. After the meeting is called to order, Sam Adams arises to present a resolution: "As the town have determined at a late meeting legally assembled," he reads, "that they will to the utmost of their power prevent the landing of the tea, the question be now put,—whether this body are absolutely determined that the tea now arrived in Captain Hall's vessel shall be returned to the place from whence it came."

There is not one dissenting voice. The resolution is loudly acclaimed.

Faneuil Hall is already jammed, but more and more people are gathering outside, clamoring to get in. It is voted to adjourn to Old South Meeting House where there is more space. Within the hour five thousand find seats in the church. Sam Adams again repeats his motion and adds, "Is it the firm resolution of this body that the tea shall not only be sent back, but that no duty shall be paid thereon?"

The shouts of applause are heartwarming to the patriot leader. Speech after speech follows—some bitter, others calm, but all advising the people to abstain from any violence. Dr. Young asks for permission to speak and fearlessly voices opposition to the landing of the tea. Further, he says, he thinks the only way to get rid of the obnoxious stuff is to toss it overboard.

The meeting adjourns until three o'clock, in hopes

that the tea agents will then come forward with some new proposals for solving the present crisis.

Both the twenty-three-year-old owner of the *Dartmouth,* the Quaker Francis Rotch, and James Hall, captain of the ship, are in the audience when the meeting reconvenes. Rotch arises and protests the proceedings. A resolution is immediately passed that if Rotch attempts to unload the tea, it will be "at his own peril." A warning is issued to Captain Hall not to allow any of his cargo to be put ashore; he is also ordered to bring his ship from Long Wharf this very afternoon and tie up at Griffin's Wharf.

It is proposed—and voted unanimously—that a twenty-four-hour watch be posted beside the ship. The men will work in shifts, twenty-five on duty at all times. Captain Ezekiel Cheever is appointed to command the watch this first night. The audience is advised that if the guard should be attacked, that if there is any violence, they will be alerted by the church bells. Should the attack occur during the day, the bells will ring wildly; if by night, the bells will toll solemnly.

John Hancock announces that he has had word from the tea agents. They have asked for one more day in which to draw up their proposals. Grudgingly, consent is given.

Late in the afternoon news reaches the gathering that Governor Hutchinson has ordered his justices of the peace to be on duty throughout the night to avoid any uprising from the patriots. Thoroughly angered, the audience calls this an insult. It is moved to adjourn until tomorrow morning.

Down along Griffin's Wharf, several hours later, the

guard is mustered, armed with muskets and bayonets. Because most of the volunteers are militia officers, they keep strict military discipline. Every half hour the word is passed from guard to guard, "All is well."

Although today's meeting had specified that the watch would be instituted to prevent any violence, everyone knows there is a dual purpose. The men are walking their beats to make certain that not one chest of tea is secretly landed.

8
The Rift
Widens

Once again, on the morning of November 30, the citizens crowd into Old South Meeting House to continue deliberation about the tea crisis. Selectman John Scollay arises and asks permission to read a letter he has received from the agents, now living out at Castle William.

The agents insist that they have no right to send the tea back to London. However, they are willing to store it, they say, until they can communicate with the East India Company and receive further orders.

Such a proposal is declared completely unsatisfactory. The gathering refuses to even consider it.

Suddenly Sheriff Stephen Greenleaf appears at the door of the meetinghouse and walks hurriedly to the platform. Interrupting a speech by one of the patriots, the burly law officer draws a paper from his pocket, announcing that he has a proclamation from Governor Hutchinson who, like the agents, has left Boston for the safety of his home in Milton.

Some laugh; others boo. But Sam Adams steps forward and pleads for fairness. Hear the man out, Adams urges.

In a loud voice the sheriff reads:

> In faithfulness to my trust, and as his Majesty's representative within the Province, I am bound to bear testimony against this violation of the laws, and I warn and exhort you and require you, and each of you thus unlawfully assembled forthwith, to disperse and to surcease all further unlawful proceedings at your utmost peril.
>
> Given under my hand, at Milton, in the Province aforesaid, the 30th of November, 1773, and in the fourteenth year of his Majesty's reign.
>
> T. Hutchinson
>
> By his Excellency's command,
>   Thomas Flucker, Secretary

An angry chorus of hisses and shouts follows. It is voted to ignore the Governor's proclamation and the sheriff hastily retreats.

In the audience this morning is the artist John Singleton Copley. He has friends both among the Whigs and
the Tories, and hates violence of any kind. Copley has
been horrified by the anger exhibited here today. He
senses the restlessness and the frustration which seems to
be sweeping through the crowd. On a sudden impulse,
the artist arises and asks for the floor.

Everyone knows that Copley is sympathetic toward
his in-laws, the Clarkes. Nonetheless, most people respect
him as a man of moderation, nonpartisan in his political
views. He is granted permission to speak.

The artist, seeking some sort of compromise, suggests
that he will go to Castle William and prevail on the tea
agents to appear at this meeting. If they agree, he wants
to be certain they will be "treated with civility while in
the meeting . . . and their persons be safe till their return
to the place from whence they should come."

The matter is put to a vote and the agents' safety is
assured. Copley then asks for two hours' time in which to
seek out the men and bring them back. Surely a face-to-
face meeting with this audience will bring about some
sort of understanding. The motion passes and the meeting temporarily adjourns.

The wind is blowing in sharp gusts across the bay
as Copley steps into the boat that will take him to Castle
William. Despite his fear of the sea, the artist knows the
importance of his mission and rows confidently across the
water. If only he can persuade the agents to return with
him and talk sensibly with the leaders!

His hopes are doomed. The agents indignantly refuse
his proposals. They prefer to remain safely behind the

fortifications at Castle William, they say. All negotiations will be carried on by letter.

Copley argues so long with his Tory friends that he is very late in returning to Old South. As he nears the meetinghouse, he can hear rising tones of an orator haranguing the crowd. An angry roar erupts. Hesitantly, he pauses at the door, gathering all his courage to face the audience which he suspects is now impatient at his delay.

When the speaker on the platform sees Copley coming down the side aisle, he stops in mid-sentence. There is a noticeable rustle as five thousand people turn in their seats to get a look at the artist. Upon reaching the platform Copley says he knows he has exceeded the time allowed him, but he hopes they will consider the difficulty of getting to Castle William by boat.

There is hostile silence. Each person in the room wonders why the artist has returned alone.

Copley explains that the agents have refused to appear, not from fear of being attacked, but because they feel their presence will solve nothing. However, he adds, they renew their offer to store the tea, but still maintain it is not in their power to return the cargo to the East India Company.

After reporting this message, the artist appeals to the gathering. If the agents are forced to return the tea, they will be ruined financially. Can't this fact be taken into consideration, he begs.

"Never, never!" the people shout.

An accusation is then made that the agents are merely tools of Governor Hutchinson, acting under his orders. It is voted unanimously that the indecisive answer which artist Copley has brought back is completely unsatisfactory.

Now it seems there is only one alternative.

Owner Francis Rotch is called to the platform. The Whig leaders demand that he order Captain Hall to sail out of the harbor with the tea aboard the *Dartmouth* and return to London. Grudgingly Rotch promises to see what he can do about getting a pass from the customs officers. Similar promises are extracted from the owners of the ships which have not yet arrived.

Next, plans are made to continue the watch at Griffin's Wharf "until the vessels leave the harbor." Volunteers are urged to sign up at Edes and Gill's print shop for guard duty. Before adjournment Paul Revere asks for the floor. He proposes, he says, to find five more experienced riders who will be willing at any hour to mount their horses and spread the alarm through the countryside, should there be any trouble at the wharf.

His boldness is endorsed by loud cheers. Sam Adams smiles to himself. He will continue to protest the tea tax by every legal, every reasonable means possible. But he knows that if the time comes when something more drastic is necessary the people of Boston now stand firmly behind the patriot leaders.

9
Suspense
Mounts

Tempers grow shorter as the days wear on. Public anger toward the tea agents rises. Boston is swept up in a fury the town has not known for many years.

On Thursday, December 2, the ship *Eleanor*, commanded by Captain James Bruce, sails into the harbor and anchors at Griffin's Wharf. A few days later it is joined by the brig *Beaver* in charge of Captain Hezekiah

Coffin. There is little taking place along the waterfront these days—none of the usual feverish activity. The ships' crews stay out of sight, although hundreds of spectators gather along the wharf to stare at the hated ships. Notices are posted around town signed "The People," stating that anyone who tries to unload the vessels will be treated "as Wretches unworthy to live and will be made victims of our just Resentment."

Meanwhile, rumor after rumor is reaching Governor Hutchinson at his country estate in Milton. He hears that the patriots are urging the shipowners to send their vessels back to England with the tea still aboard. It is quite understandable that the owners are not pleased at being caught in the midst of an argument between the governor and the patriots. Every day spent in Boston's port is costly. The crews' wages must be paid; valuable time is being lost. There may be a temptation to try and slip out past Castle William without the required clearance papers.

The governor acts to forestall any such notion. He directs Admiral Montague to put the British armed men-of-war *Active* and *Kingfisher* on patrol duty. To Colonel Leslie, who commands the British troops stationed at Castle William, he sends written orders not to allow any vessel to pass the guns of the fortress without official permission from himself. Hutchinson still believes the leaders of the protest will back down, that there will be no trouble. After the twenty-day waiting period has elapsed, the customs officers can board the ships and remove the tea chests.

Though the governor is not fully aware of the serious

intents of the Whigs, there are many in Boston who are. John Andrews, a prominent merchant, writes a friend in early December: " 'Twould puzzle any person to purchase a pair of pistols in town as they are all bought up, with a full determination to repell force by force."

Over in the little house on Queen Street, John Adams' wife, Abigail, expresses the sentiments of the town in a letter to her dear friend, Mercy Warren, down in Plymouth. On December 5 she writes:

> The tea, that baneful weed, is arrived. Great and I hope effectual opposition has been made to the landing of it . . . . The flame is kindled and like lightning it catches from soul to soul. Although the mind is shocked at the thought of shedding human blood, more especially the blood of our countrymen, and a civil war is of all wars the most dreadful, such is the present spirit that prevails that if once they are made desperate, many, very many of our heroes will spend their lives in the cause. I tremble when I think what may be the direful consequences, and in this town must the scene of the action lie. My heart beats at every whistle I hear, and I dare not express half my fears.

People talk of nothing else during these tense days. The newspapers are full of stories about the tea. From surrounding towns come resolutions urging the citizens of Boston to stand firm. The Committee of Correspondence in nearby Leicester writes:

> Go on as you have begun; and do not suffer any of the teas already come or coming to be landed, or pay one farthing of duty. You may depend on our aid when needed.

Further encouragement comes from Worcester. In a legal town meeting the town resolved "that we will not buy, sell, use or in any way be concerned with India teas of any kind, imported from Great Britain, until the unrighteous act imposing a duty thereon be repealed."

The *Gazette* continues its attacks upon the governor. In the December 13 issue of the newspaper, the editors write:

TO MR. HUTCHINSON

When a man in public station is first found tripping in his duty to his Sovereign, or against the Majesty of the People, he is sure to be advised of it (in a free state), first by distant hints and gentle murmurs! If he still continues in the commission of his faults, he is advised in plainer language! But when he is found incorrigible in every step he has taken (as is your case) he is assuredly dealt with as the nature of his crimes requires! Strong corrosives are then thrown in, with a view, no doubt, to get rid of such a pestilence as speedily as possible. . . .

On this same day the Boston Committee of Correspondence holds a lengthy session with members from the five neighboring towns of Dorchester, Brookline, Roxbury, Charlestown, and Cambridge. A letter from the Philadelphia Committee is reported. It reads: "Our tea consignees have all resigned, and you need not fear, the tea will not be landed here nor at New York. All that we fear is that you will shrink at Boston. May God give you virtue enough to save the liberties of your country."

Time is growing very short. Although the secretary reports in his minutes that "no business transacted matter

of record," this is not the accurate situation. Secret plans must be made, in case the ships do not leave the harbor.

Francis Rotch is summoned before the committee and asked why he has not kept his promise to send the *Dartmouth* with its cargo of tea back to London. He explains that it is not in his power to do so, that he has no clearance for his ship.

Sam Adams speaks firmly. "The ship must go," he asserts, "the people of Boston and the neighboring towns absolutely require and expect it."

Since the *Dartmouth* was first to arrive in Boston, the committee believes that if Rotch can be persuaded to send his ship back to London without unloading the tea, the owners of the *Eleanor* and the *Beaver* will follow his lead. The protest against the tax will have been won.

After Rotch is dismissed, Adams points out, however, that the committee must have an alternative course of action if the ships do not leave. The idea of destroying the tea is advanced again and finds enthusiastic acceptance among the members. The Sons of Liberty can be counted on to participate, says Adams, though emphasis must be placed on having volunteers who are little known.

Someone suggests that the participants disguise themselves as Mohawk Indians and smear their faces with soot or charcoal to conceal their identity. The men chosen must be completely trustworthy. Not one single leaf of tea may be taken off the ship by any individual. Otherwise the action will become a robbery rather than an act of protest. Each man, too, must be sworn to secrecy.

With resentment and anger now at fever pitch, Adams feels there will be little trouble in finding three men to lead the volunteers aboard the *Dartmouth*, the *Eleanor*, and the *Beaver*. The destruction of the tea chests, it is agreed, must be done quietly, efficiently. No damage must occur . . . the vessels should be left as shipshape as they are when the Indians arrive on board. Docks will be swept clean and inspected by the ship's leader before the men leave.

There will be one last mass meeting at Old South on December 16. Rotch will be given a final opportunity to order his ship back to London with the tea in its hold. If the owner secures the necessary permission, Sam Adams will simply say to the audience, "Now may God help my country" and the crisis will be resolved peacefully. However, if Rotch fails to secure clearance papers, there is no other course to follow. The hated tea must be destroyed. The prearranged signal for the volunteer Mohawks to go into action will be Adams' statement, "This meeting can do nothing more to save the country."

Before the committee adjourns, it is decided to hold another mass meeting tomorrow. A formal demand will be made; the shipowners must order their vessels back to England.

On the morning of December 14 handbills are passed out on the streets of Boston. They challenge

> Friends! Brethren! Countrymen! The perfidious act of your reckless enemies to render ineffectual the late resolves of the body of the people, demands your assembling at the Old South Meeting House, precisely at ten o'clock this day, at which time the bells will ring!

No other announcement is necessary. By the specified hour the church is filled with several thousand local citizens and hundreds from the surrounding towns. Sam Adams and the Committees of Correspondence are trying every peaceful means they can devise in order to dissolve the dispute. Rotch is called to the platform and asked whether he has secured the necessary clearance for the *Dartmouth*. His evasive answer makes it obvious that the owner is stalling for time. The audience is angered.

Legally, no ship can leave a port until it has been unloaded. Since the tea is part of the *Dartmouth's* cargo, it must be landed before the ship can be given a clearance. Furthermore, British law states that no ship can re-enter an English port until it has discharged its cargo.

After some argument, Rotch promises to call on the customs officer this very afternoon. Once again the harassed owner is warned there are only two days left. The deadline is fast approaching, and all Boston is taut with suspense.

Will the ship sail peacefully—or is there trouble to come?

10
Crisis
in Old
South

A cold drizzle, steady and chilling, drips from the clouds that hover over Boston on this morning of December 16, 1773. Feverish excitement grips the town. Everyone knows that today is the deadline —the last day it will be possible for Francis Rotch to order his ship *Dartmouth* back to England with the tea cargo still in its hold. By tomorrow the twenty-day period of grace will have expired. Royal customs officials can legally enter the ship, take off the tea chests and put them in storage to be sold later at public auction.

A mass meeting has been called for ten o'clock this morning. Despite the weather, no one wants to miss it. From church steeples the bells ring, loud and insistent, calling everyone to Old South. Hundreds of men hasten through the narrow streets and alleys, all heading for the meetinghouse. Womenfolk, left behind, peer through the tiny paned windows of their homes to watch as the crowds hurry by.

Since early morning Boston Neck, the only land approach to the town, has been jammed with carts and wagons, drays and chaises. From the outlying villages they streamed across the narrow strip. People are coming from as far away as twenty miles—proof that Sam Adams' Committee of Correspondence has done a good job in arousing the support of the surrounding towns.

By the appointed hour some five thousand are inside Old South. From the ropewalks, the blacksmiths' shops, the wharves, and the sailmakers' lofts, men have come to participate in this momentous gathering. Not all the audience is dressed in drab homespun and gray leather, however. Here and there are bright satin waistcoats and neatly powdered wigs, signifying that many of the town's wealthier citizens are in sympathy with today's assembly.

Outside the meetinghouse the crowds milling about part courteously as the Whig leaders make their way to the door. Red-cloaked Sam Adams is in the lead, his thinning gray hair tossed by the blustering wind. Following closely behind are John Hancock, Dr. Joseph Warren, Dr. Thomas Young, and Will Molineux. There's a buzz of excitement as the leaders thread their way to the front. After the men seat themselves in high-backed chairs on the platform, the noise dies down to an expectant hush.

Sam Adams calls the meeting to order. Will Francis Rotch please come forward? he asks.

The young man hesitates for a moment, sensing the hostility of the crowd. Then he walks slowly to the platform and reports that a clearance for his ship has been refused by the customs officer.

The leaders on the platform confer. Rotch is told that they still seek a peaceful means of resolving the crisis. As a last resort the *Dartmouth*'s owner is directed to apply to Governor Hutchinson for a passport that will allow his ship to sail out past Castle William and back to London.

Rotch reminds the audience that the governor has retired to his country estate at Milton. That is seven miles away. It will take some time for him to travel out there and back.

A delay in the proceedings is inevitable. Sam Adams announces an adjournment. The meeting, he says, will reconvene at three o'clock this afternoon to hear Rotch's answer.

Long before the specified time, a large crowd has gathered around the meetinghouse. There's much elbowing and pushing to get inside. People shove their way toward the front door. Already the main floor is packed; the boxlike pews are overflowing. More edge up toward the double tiers of galleries, trying to get a seat on one of the benches. Some two thousand can't get in and they stand outside in the chilling rain.

The audience waits quietly. There's no loud talking

or shouting, only the low murmur of whispered conversations. Promptly at three o'clock the Whig leaders come into the church and take their places on the platform. Sam Adams calls the meeting to order and announces that Mr. Rotch has not yet returned with his answer. There will be speeches while they wait, he adds.

Meanwhile, those who have agreed to participate in the tea party—if it occurs—are gathering at the pre-appointed places. In the back room of a store on Fort Hill men smear their faces with soot, sling Indian blankets over their shoulders, and procure axes which they laughingly refer to as "tomahawks." For the most part these volunteers are apprentices, journeymen, carpenters, farmers, and blacksmiths who have been told that if identified, they may be tried for treason. Yet they are anxious to join in.

Printer Benjamin Edes has offered his house on Cornhill for others who have volunteered to disguise themselves as Mohawks tonight. Behind barred doors the men put on tattered clothes—parts of blankets, torn jackets, whatever they can improvise. Some rub red paint on their faces. Others use charcoal dust—anything that will conceal their identity.

In an adjoining room, Edes' twelve-year-old son, Peter, is making punch. Edes has requested that Peter use their best bowl—the china one, elaborately decorated with Chinese flowers, trees, and gardens. Though Peter is not allowed to meet any of the guests, Edes explains to his son that nothing is too good for his friends this afternoon. Once the punch is mixed, Peter knocks on the locked door. It's ready, he calls.

Benjamin Edes opens the door only far enough to take the bowl, then locks it again. His guests fill their tankards and drink up while they wait for the prearranged signal. The printer makes out a list of those who are here; however, their identity must never be known. He hides the paper in a secret drawer of his desk.

As the hours drag by, the speeches continue at Old South. Some urge caution, but this brings forth noisy cat-calls. Sam Adams mounts the pulpit and asks whether the tea shall be landed.

Cries of "No! No! Never!" resound through the meetinghouse.

Someone shouts, "Who knows how tea will mingle with salt water?" There's a ripple of laughter and the crowd starts applauding.

Back in the east gallery Josiah Quincy, Jr. jumps to his feet. As a young lawyer practicing in Boston, he has been very active in the protest against the Tea Tax. Now Quincy can no longer contain himself. "Whoever supposes that shouts and hosannas will terminate the trials of the day entertains a childish fancy," he admonishes the audience. "We must be grossly ignorant of the importance and value of the prize for which we contend; we must be equally ignorant of the power of those who have combined against us . . . to hope that we shall end this controversy without the sharpest conflicts, to flatter ourselves that popular resolves, popular harangues, popular acclamations and popular vapor will vanquish our foes. . . . Let us weigh and consider before we advance to those measures which must bring on the most trying and terrific struggle this country ever saw."

Down on the main floor old Harrison Gray rises. In a voice trembling with age he warns "the young gentleman in the gallery" against the use of such impetuous language.

Answering Gray, Quincy replies, "If the old gentleman on the floor intends by his warning to 'the young gentleman in the gallery' to utter only a friendly voice in the spirit of paternal advice, I thank him."

There is silence for a moment.

Drawing in his breath, Quincy continues, "If his object is to terrify and intimidate, I despise him. . . . I see the clouds now rise thick and fast upon our horizon, the thunder roll, and the lightning play, and to that God who rides the whirlwind and directs the storm, I commit my country."

Someone below the gallery shouts out, "The hand is to the plow. There must be no looking back!"

Loud applause follows. Sam Adams raps sharply to restore order. Once again he asks whether the tea shall be allowed to land. There is not one murmur of dissent. The vote is unanimous.

It is now after five o'clock and the meetinghouse has grown quite dark. The sexton pushes his way down the side aisles, lighting the candles in brass sconces along the walls. The speeches continue.

At five forty-five Rotch returns. His face is tense as he shoulders through the crowd toward the front platform. He talks with Sam Adams for a moment and then turns toward the sea of faces. In a halting voice the *Dartmouth*'s owner reports that Governor Hutchinson has refused permission for the tea ships to leave the harbor, that "for the honor of the laws and from duty towards the King, he could not grant the permit until the vessel was regularly cleared."

Hisses and catcalls fill the church. Adams holds up his hand for quiet. Once more, he asks Rotch whether he will send the ship back to England with the tea still aboard.

Rotch throws up his arms in horror, saying that if he did such a thing it would be his own ruin.

The audience waits—rigid, silent.

With deliberate steps Sam Adams mounts the pulpit.

In a voice quavering with excitement, he says: "This meeting can do nothing more to save the country."

From somewhere in the gallery there's a shrill whistle. Outside a chorus of ear-splitting yells rents the air. Near the front door a group of Indians suddenly appears. The audience gasps. Are they being attacked by red men?

Shouts ring out.

"Boston harbor a tea pot tonight!"

"To Griffin's Wharf!"

"The Mohawks are come!"

"Every man to his tent!"

While the crowd streams out of the church, the Whig leaders stand side by side on the platform. None moves toward the door. There's a quiet look of triumph on Sam Adams' face.

11
The Tea
Party

Outside, the rain has stopped. It is colder now. The wind gusting across the harbor has a sharp tinge. But skies are clearing. A full moon seems to dart back and forth between the fast-moving clouds.

The people pouring out of Old South are amazed at the sight of some fifty Mohawk Indians clustered along Milk Street. Now the yelling and the war whoops have

ceased. The Mohawks pair up two-by-two and march off
in orderly fashion. More join the procession as they pass
Fort Hill. There is no hilarity; only the steady tramp of
feet echoes on the cobblestones. Their mission is deadly
serious.

As the Indians near Griffin's Wharf, younger men and
boys join in behind the marchers. Though the leaders had
specified that tonight's work must be done by those "not
much known in Town and not liable to be easily recog-
nized," there are some who are more bold than discreet.
They have not taken time to blacken their faces, yet they
know the risk is great. If their identity is known, they
may be arrested and tried for treason. Sam Adams and
his friends have done their work well. These volunteers
prize their freedom more than they do their own lives.

When the Mohawks reach the dock, they separate
into three groups. Each group is led by a captain who has
been well-versed in tonight's procedure. There is no con-
fusion as the men clamber over the sides of the ships.

Not one volunteer has any suspicion that a British
official is watching every move. Admiral Montague is
spending the night with his Tory friend, Mr. Coffin, who
lives at the head of Griffin's Wharf. The sound of march-
ing feet brought the Admiral to an upstairs window. As
the Mohawks swarm onto the ships' decks, the Royal
officer surmises what is about to happen. However, he
makes no move to stop them.

Along the wharf a large crowd gathers, many having
followed the Indians from Old South. Not a word is
spoken. The people watch in approving silence.

Captain Lendell Pitts is in charge of the Mohawks

who board the brig *Beaver*. Finding the foredeck deserted, he directs one of his men to locate the ship's mate and ask for keys to the hold, as well as some lanterns. Inform the mate that if the crew causes no trouble, there will be no damage, adds Pitts.

The messenger soon returns with the necessary keys, followed by a bosun with lanterns. Captain Pitts orders the hold unlocked and details some of the Mohawks to jump down. Chests will be passed up, attached to the winch, and hoisted onto the deck. Other volunteers are to open the chests and dump both tea and containers into the harbor.

Within minutes the hoisting tackles begin to creak. The great boxes come swaying up. Men with hatchets smash them open. They find that the tea has been wrapped in heavy canvas. It is easy to split the wood but the wrapping causes more difficulty. No one stops for even a moment. Carefully, methodically they continue shattering the chests. Over the offshore rail go the broken containers and the tea.

Silence prevails as the men work swiftly. The only noise is the creak of the winches, the sound of wood being ripped apart, followed by a soft swish as the tea hits the water.

Less than a quarter of a mile away His Majesty's men-of-war, the *Active* and the *Kingfisher*, ride at anchor. No sound comes from these vessels though the men on the tea ships' decks are aware that the guns point directly toward them. Will they be fired on? No matter. There's a job to be done. No one wastes time worrying about what might happen.

One of the volunteers, George Robert Twelves Hewes, watches a fellow worker on the *Beaver* with a wary eye. What is Charles O'Connor doing? Hewes wonders. Is he trying to steal some tea? O'Connor's movements are odd. Every little while he works his hands up and down his pantaloons and along the lining of his coat.

When Hewes goes to Captain Pitts to voice his suspicions, O'Connor jumps over the side of the brig onto the wharf. There's a cry of "East Indian" and Hewes is off in pursuit. The offender is grabbed by the coattails and pulled back aboard the ship. Several Mohawks relieve O'Connor of the hidden tea as well as the obnoxious pantaloons. Then with a couple of kicks they toss him back on the wharf. O'Connor recognizes Hewes during the scuffle and threatens "to complain to the Governor." Angered, Hewes shouts back, "You'd better make your will first" and doubles his fists as O'Connor flees.

Once all the chests have been dumped overboard, Pitts calls for brooms. The deck is to be swept clean; the ship must be left exactly as it was when the men came aboard. Spilled tea, shreds of canvas, splinters of wood— all must be tossed over the side.

Captain Pitts then directs one of the Mohawks to go below and bring the mate topside. When the man appears, Pitts hands him the keys to the hold. Please look around, he insists, to see that no damage has been done. The mate has no complaints. It's all shipshape, he admits, somewhat unhappily.

Much the same procedure has been followed on the *Dartmouth* and the *Eleanor*. Each ship carried one hundred and fourteen chests of tea. After all three hundred and forty-two chests are dumped into the harbor, the Mohawks reassemble on the wharf, lining up two-by-two. They are ordered to remove their shoes and empty any small shred of tea into the water. The three captains pass up and down the file of men, inspecting each one carefully.

Now that their job is finished, the volunteers march off in a double line. Those with axes and hatchets shoulder them like rifles. The crowd, gathered on the wharf, falls back to open a pathway. When the retreating Indians pass Mr. Coffin's house, Admiral Montague puts up a window and calls out:

"Well, boys, you have had a fine pleasant evening for your Indian caper, haven't you? But mind, you have to pay the fiddler yet!"

"Oh, never mind," retorts Pitts. "Never mind, Squire! Just come out here, if you please, and we'll settle the bill in two minutes!"

Shouts of laughter ripple through the ranks of Mohawks. The Admiral slams down the window. Someone pulls out a fife and the company marches off to the spirited tune of "Yankee Doodle."

Back on Milk Street the groups break up. Each man heads quietly for home. The mission is completed. There's no need to linger.

By ten o'clock the streets are deserted.

12
The Day After

The tension, the suspense which has filled the town these past two months is now dispelled. Last night's episode has left the Whigs in a jubilant mood. By this one daring act, they have proven to Royal authorities that they cannot be intimidated, that liberty and freedom are uppermost in their minds. What Parliament's reaction will be no one knows. There may be drastic acts of reprisal. But on this morning of December

17 no one is particularly worried about this possibility.

A meeting of the Committee of Correspondence is called for nine o'clock this morning in Faneuil Hall. When all are present, Chairman Sam Adams confides there was one unexpected consequence as a result of last night's project. Before dawn he had been informed that the incoming tide had played tricks. A fringe of tea was discovered all around the shore line at the high water mark. A party of volunteers was stirred up. They turned out in boats, drenching the leaves with oars and paddles. By sunup, there was not one dry leaf of tea.

The members applaud Adams' quick-thinking action.

The chairman suggests that the people of New York and Philadelphia must be informed of what has happened in Boston. Several riders have volunteered to carry the communications to these cities. Adams names the men. The committee decides that Paul Revere is best qualified. He's an expert horseman and is familiar with the rugged Post Road.

To save precious time, Adams has already written the dispatch. He hopes the Committee will approve. After detailing what Boston has done he adds:

> We are in a perfect jubilee. Not a Tory in the whole community can find the least fault with our proceedings. . . . The spirit of the people throughout the country is to be described by no terms in my power. Their conduct last night surprised the admiral and English gentlemen, who observed that these were not a mob of disorderly rabble (as they had reported), but men of sense, coolness and intrepidity.

Within the hour, Paul Revere is booted and spurred. The communications are safely tucked into his saddlebag and he's off across Boston Neck, galloping swiftly along the Post Road leading down to New York City.

Meanwhile, out at Milton Hill, Governor Hutchinson is stunned by the news of what took place last night at Griffin's Wharf. Such drastic action had never occurred to him.

Since late in November he has been living at his country estate. His Tory friends in Boston had not impressed him sufficiently with the determination of these Whigs. He thought they were only bluffing, that if the tea could not be shipped back to London, they would back down. Then after the twenty days had elapsed, his customs officials would seize the cargo and offer it at auction. The governor had never considered the possibility that Sam Adams and his friends would not give in at the last moment. Now, he has the agonizing job of explaining to Parliament and the East India officials what has happened.

Though the Whigs are rejoicing over the boldness of last night's action, the Tories are infuriated. One writes a friend in England that "The crime of the Bostonians was a compound of the grossest injury and insult. It was an act of the highest insolence towards government, such as mildness itself cannot overlook or forgive. The injustice of the deed was also most atrocious . . . ."

Lawyer John Adams was in Plymouth yesterday trying a case in court there. He arrives on horseback at noon today and hears from his wife, Abigail, what took place last night. John has sometimes disapproved of the more radical actions of his second cousin, Sam. Yet this event leaves him overjoyed. The act had involved no violence, no revenge on any individual. It was Parliament that was being attacked on a matter of principle. To his diary he confides:

> This is the most magnificent Movement of all. There is a Dignity, a Majesty, a Sublimity, in this last effort of the Patriots, that I greatly admire. The People should never rise, without doing something to be remembered—something notable. And striking. This Destruction of the Tea is so bold, so daring, so firm, intrepid and inflexible, and it must have so important Consequences, and so lasting, that I can't but consider it as an Epocha in History.

Epilogue

One week later the Committee of Correspondence met in Faneuil Hall. There had been alarming reports around town that anyone known to have taken part in the daring performance at Griffin's Wharf would be arrested and executed for treason. Members of the committee signed a solemn pledge:

The subscribers do engage to exert our utmost influence to support and vindicate each other, and

any person or persons who may be likely to suffer
for any noble efforts they may have made to save
their country, by defeating the operations of the
British Parliament, expressly designed to extort a
revenue from the Colonies against their support.

On January 20, 1774, the merchant ship *Hayley* arrived in London, bringing news of the Boston Tea Party.
King George III and members of Parliament were
shocked. Shock turned to fury. Parliament acted accordingly.

Late in March the Boston Port Bill was passed; on
March 31 King George affixed his signature. No ship
could enter the harbor after June 1, 1774, until the East
India Company was compensated for its losses. England
was determined not only to humiliate the patriots but to
starve Boston into submission.

A military general, George Gage, replaced Thomas
Hutchinson. Four thousand British troops arrived and
were quartered in town. The harbor was filled with Royal
warships, ready to fire on the first vessel that attempted
to pass Castle William.

Parliament was confident that such drastic measures
would bring the colonists to their senses and force them
once again to be dependent upon the mother country.
Instead, Boston greeted the reprisal with defiance. Sam
Adams wrote an acquaintance in London that the people
would "sustain the shock with dignity and . . . gloriously
defeat the designs of their enemies."

In New York, Philadelphia, and Charleston, the tea
agents had all resigned under public pressure, and the
ships returned to London filled with their original cargo.

The colonies were beginning to unite now, as never before. Revolt was inevitable, a revolt that was eventually to be climaxed by American independence.

The identity of the participants in the action of December 16, 1773, remained a secret for more than sixty years. Finally, in 1835 Benjamin Thatcher published a book entitled *Traits of the Tea Party*. He had secured from relatives of the Benjamin Edes family the list the printer had locked in his desk. Substantiated by nine of the volunteers still living, Mr. Thatcher published the first known list of those who took part in the famous tea party. They are:

George R. T. Hewes	Ebenezer Stevens
Joseph Shed	Josiah Wheeler
John Crane	Thomas Urann
S. Coolidge	Adam Collson
Joseph Payson	Nicholas Campbell
James Brewer	John Russell
Thomas Bolter	Thomas Porter
Edward Proctor	William Hendley
Samuel Sloper	Benjamin Rice
Thomas Gerrish	Samuel Gore
Nathaniel Green	Nathaniel Frothingham
Benjamin Simpson	Moses Grant
Joseph Eayres	Peter Slater
Joseph Lee	James Starr
William Molineux	Abraham Tower

Paul Revere
John Spurr
Thomas Moore
Samuel Howard
Matthew Loring
Thomas Spear
Daniel Ingoldson
Richard Hunnewell
John Hooton
Jonathan Hunnewell
Thomas Chase
Thomas Melvill
Henry Purkitt
Edward C. Howe

William Pierce
William Russell
T. Gammell
———— McIntosh
Dr. Thomas Young
Joshua Wyeth
Edward Dolbear
———— Martin
Samuel Peck
Lendell Pitts
Samuel Sprague
Benjamin Clarke
Richard Hunnewell, Jr.
John Prince

Many people claimed their ancestors had participated in the Boston Tea Party, although there is no real evidence to support their claims. However, Thatcher added these names to the list which he states were "derived principally from family tradition."

Nathaniel Barber
Samuel Barnard
Henry Bass
Edward Bates
Nathaniel Bradlee
David Bradlee
Josiah Bradlee
Thomas Bradlee
Seth Ingersoll Brown
Stephen Bruce
Benjamin Burton
George Carleton
Gilbert Colesworthy
John Cochran
Gershom Collier

Jeremiah Williams
Thomas Williams
Nathaniel Willis
John Fulton
Samuel Hammond
John Hicks
Samuel Hobbs
Thomas Hunstable
Abraham Hunt
David Kinnison
Amos Lincoln
Thomas Machin
Archibald Macneil
John May
———— Mead

James Foster Condy
Samuel Cooper
Thomas Dana, Jr.
Robert Davis
Joseph Eaton
———— Eckley
William Etheridge
Samuel Fenno
Samuel Foster
James Swan
John Truman
Isaac Williams
David Williams

Anthony Morse
Eliphalet Newell
Joseph Pearse Palmer
Jonathan Parker
John Peters
Samuel Pitts
Henry Prentiss
John Randall
Joseph Roby
Phineas Stearns
Robert Sessions
Elisha Story

Bibliography

Adams, James Truslow. *Provincial Society, 1690–1763.* New York: Macmillan Co., 1927.

Adams, James Truslow. *Revolutionary New England: 1691–1776.* Boston: Atlantic Monthly Press, 1923.

Adams, John. *Diary and Autobiography.* Edited by L. H. Butterfield. Volumes 2, 3. Cambridge, Mass.: Harvard University Press, Belknap Press, 1961.

Andrews, John. *Letters of John Andrews, 1772–1776.* Cambridge, Mass.: John Wilson & Sons, 1866.

Anthony, Katharine. *First Lady of the Revolution: The Life of Mercy Otis Warren.* Garden City, N.Y.: Doubleday & Company, 1958.

Beach, Stewart. *Samuel Adams: The Fateful Years, 1764–1776.* New York: Dodd, Mead & Co., 1965.

Boardman, Samuel L. *Peter Edes, A Biography.* Bangor, Maine: Privately printed for the De Burians, 1901.

Bridenbaugh, Carl. *The Colonial Craftsman.* New York: New York University Press, 1950.

Brown, Alice, *Mercy Warren.* New York: Charles Scribner's Sons, 1896.

Buckingham, Joseph T. *Specimens of Newspaper Literature with Personal Memoirs, Anecdotes, and Reminiscences.* Volume I. Boston: Charles C. Little and James Brown, 1850.

Callahan, North. *Royal Raiders: The Tories of the American Revolution.* Indianapolis: The Bobbs-Merrill Co., 1963.

Chamberlain, Allen. *Beacon Hill.* Boston: Houghton Mifflin Co., 1925.

Commager, Henry Steele and Richard B. Morris, eds. *The Spirit of Seventy-Six.* New York: Harper & Row, 1958.

Comstock, Sarah. *Roads to the Revolution.* New York: Macmillan Company, 1928.

Crawford, Mary Caroline. *Old Boston Days and Ways.* Boston: Little, Brown & Co., 1913.

Crawford, Mary Caroline. *Old Boston in Colonial Days.* Boston: The Page Company, 1908.

Cunningham, Anne Rowe, ed. *Letters and Diary of John Rowe.* Boston: W. B. Clarke Company, 1903.

Dexter, Elisabeth Anthony. *Colonial Women of Affairs.* Cambridge, Mass.: Riverside Press, 1924.

Drake, Francis S. *Tea Leaves: A Collection of Letters and Documents Relating to the Shipment of Tea to the American Colonies in 1773.* Boston: A. O. Crane, 1884.

Drake, Samuel A. *Old Boston Taverns.* Boston: Cupples, Upham, & Co., 1886.

Drake, Samuel A. *Old Landmarks and Historic Personages of Boston.* Boston: Little, Brown & Co., 1873.

Drake, Samuel A. *Our Colonial Homes.* Boston: Lee and Shepard, Publishers, 1894.

Fisher, Sydney George. *The Struggle for American Independence.* Volume 1. Philadelphia: J. B. Lippincott Co., 1908.

Flexner, James Thomas. *John Singleton Copley.* Boston: Riverside Press, 1948.

Forbes, Esther. *The Boston Book.* Boston: Houghton Mifflin Co., 1947.

Forbes, Esther. *Paul Revere and the World He Lived In.* Boston: Houghton Mifflin Co., 1942.

Graham, Shirley. *The Story of Phillis Wheatley, Poetess of the American Revolution.* New York: Julian Messner, 1949.

Hart, Albert Bushnell, ed. *American History Told by Contemporaries.* Volume 2. New York: Macmillan Company, 1896.

Hawkes, James (supposed author). *A Retrospect of the Boston Tea Party.* New York: S. S. Bliss, printer, 1834.

Hosmer, James K. *Life of Thomas Hutchinson.* Boston: Houghton Mifflin Co., 1896.

Hosmer, James K. *Samuel Adams.* Cambridge, Mass.: Riverside Press, 1885.

Jennings, John. *Boston: Cradle of Liberty, 1630–1776.* Garden City, N.Y.: Doubleday & Co., 1947.

Jensen, Merrill. *The Founding of a Nation.* New York: Oxford University Press, 1968.

Labaree, Benjamin Woods. *The Boston Tea Party.* New York: Oxford University Press, 1964.

Mann, Albert W. *Walks and Talks About Historic Boston.* Boston: Mann Publishing Company, 1917.

Miller, John C. *Origins of the American Revolution.* Boston: Little, Brown & Co., 1943.

Miller, John C. *Sam Adams: Pioneer in Propaganda.* Boston: Little, Brown & Co., 1936.

"Minutes of the Tea Meetings," *Proceedings* of the Massachusetts Historical Society. Series 1, Volume XX. Boston: Published by the Society, 1882–1883.

Mussey, Barrows, ed. *Yankee Life by Those Who Lived It.* New York: Alfred A. Knopf, 1947.

Mott, Frank Luther. *American Journalism: A History, 1690–1960.* New York: Macmillan Co., 1962.

Schlesinger, Arthur Meier. *The Colonial Merchants and the American Revolution, 1763–1776.* New York: Columbia University Press, 1918.

Singleton, Esther, ed. *Historic Buildings of America.* New York: Dodd Mead & Co., 1907.

Tebbel, John. *The Compact History of the American Newspaper.* New York: Hawthorn Books, 1963.

Thatcher, Benjamin B. *Traits of the Tea Party.* New York: Harper & Bros., 1835.

Thwing, Annie Haven. *Crooked and Narrow Streets of Town of Boston.* Boston: Marshall Jones Co., 1920.

Truax, Rhoda. *The Doctors Warren of Boston.* Boston: Houghton Mifflin Co., 1968.

Ukers, W. H. *All About Tea.* New York: The Tea and Coffee Trade Journal Co., 1935.

Vaughan, Alden T., ed. *Chronicles of the American Revolution.* Originally compiled by Hezekiah Niles. New York: Grosset & Dunlap, 1965.

Wall, Caleb Arnold. *The Historic Boston Tea Party of December 16, 1773.* Worcester, Mass.: Press of F. S. Blanchard & Co., 1896.

Warden, G. B. *Boston, 1689–1776.* Boston: Little, Brown & Co., 1970.

Whitney, Janet. *Abigail Adams.* Boston: Little, Brown & Co., 1947.

Writer's Program. *Boston Looks Seaward: The Story of the Port, 1630–1940.* Boston: Bruce Humphries, 1941.

Index

ABOUT THE AUTHOR

Mary Kay Phelan's career as a writer began in response to questions from her two young sons. When, after a trip to Washington, she could not find a book that satisfied their demands for more information about the White House, she wrote one herself. And she has continued to write books that bring American history vividly to life. Mrs. Phelan is the author of *Four Days in Philadelphia—1776*, which tells the story of the adoption of the Declaration of Independence; *Midnight Alarm: The Story of Paul Revere's Ride; The Story of the Great Chicago Fire, 1871; Mr. Lincoln's Inaugural Journey; Probing the Unknown: The Story of Dr. Florence Sabin; Martha Berry;* and three books in the Crowell Holiday Series—*Mother's Day, The Fourth of July,* and *Election Day.*

Born in Kansas, Mrs. Phelan was graduated from DePauw University in Indiana and received her master's degree in English from Northwestern University. She has worked as an advertising copy writer and she and her husband are now involved in the production of historical films which are widely used in schools and libraries. The Phelans live in Davenport, Iowa, most of the year but enjoy their frequent travels in this country and in Europe.

ABOUT THE ILLUSTRATOR

Born in Astoria, Long Island, Frank Aloise attended Textile High School in Manhattan, where he studied advertising art. After serving in the army he resumed his education at the Art Students League, studying with the distinguished artists Reginald Marsh and John Groth. He also attended the Workshop School of Art and the School of Visual Arts.

Mr. Aloise finds that reference work and love of detail keep him happy when he is illustrating a historical book. Having previously illustrated biographies of George Washington and Nathan Hale, he especially enjoyed going back to the visually exciting and emotionally stimulating colonial period of our history.